Here's what people are saying about *shrimp*

"In *shrimp*, jason vasser-elong casts past, present, and future into the waters of fitful reckoning. His words emerge from the waves and froth, spelling out the truths behind ancestry and individuality."

— Ron Austin, professor, author and
2016 Regional Arts Commission Fellow

"jason vasser-elong's verse pulls at the very sinews of our heart muscles. With a surgeon's eye, he moves from massaging the muscle to life — 'she looks back over her tomb/ then back into the trees/ trembling to the shore' — to incisive cutting — 'beneath my skin are feathers,/ what comes out as words are really songs.' The dexterity with which he moves between subjectivities serves to create an adventurous collection; alternately gripping with suspenseful narrative, and, and at times, drenched in sorrowful, knowing lyricism. *shrimp* is an astounding debut collection."

— Treasure Shields-Redmond, poet, speaker, diversity and
inclusion coach, and social justice educator

"*shrimp* is a collection of powerful and thought-provoking poems, masterfully written, while on a quest for true identity. During his journey to discover self, jason vasser-elong draws us in with metaphors that are relatable and relevant to the issues of equality and advancement today. This collection of work is inspiring and empowering on many levels."

— Debora Grandison
writer, poet and inspirational speaker
Poetry Out Loud Regional Coordinator-STL

"Through the inviting poems in *shrimp*, jason vasser-elong includes us on his lyric quest to determine who he is and in what ways he as an individual connects with his family, his multi-racial lineage and present day society. With quiet determination, poetic poise and concision, in *shrimp* he paints for us a powerful portrait of a man unafraid to examine himself and his surroundings, whether he's in the kitchen cooking dinner or walking down Delmar Boulevard in St. Louis."

— Sally Van Doren, poet, artist and author of the poetry collection, *Promise: Poems* (2017).

Auntie Pam,

From the bottom of my heart,
I want to say thank you
for the two Beautiful garments.

Please enjoy these poems, as
they are as close to children
that I will have, lol!

I assembled this book, as a
manuscript, the weekend that
the Cameroon Royal Council gave
my name 'Elong' back to me.

Jason Carter-Elong

shrimp

shrimp

JASON VASSER-ELONG

Introduction by Michael Castro

NEW YORK

www.2leafpress.org

P.O. Box 4378
Grand Central Station
New York, New York 10163-4378
editor@2leafpress.org
www.2leafpress.org

2LEAF PRESS
is an imprint of the
Intercultural Alliance of Artists & Scholars, Inc. (IAAS),
a NY-based nonprofit 501(c)(3) organization that promotes
multicultural literature and literacy.
www.theiaas.org

Copyright © 2018 jason vasser-elong
Cover art and design: Dé-Jon Graves
Poetry editor: Sean Dillon
Book design and layout: Gabrielle David

Library of Congress Control Number: 2017963106

ISBN-13:978-1-940939-67-4 (Paperback)
ISBN-13: 978-1-940939-81-0 (eBook)

10   9   8   7   6   5   4   3   2   1

Published in the United States of America

First Edition | First Printing

2LEAF PRESS trade distribution is handled by University of Chicago Press / Chicago Distribution Center (www.press.uchicago.edu) 773.702.7010. Titles are also available for corporate, premium, and special sales. Please direct inquiries to the UCP Sales Department, 773.702.7248.

For Mary Jones and Chatty Vasser

Contents

jason vasser-elong

shrimp

Introduction

JASON VASSER-ELONG announces early on in shrimp, his debut collection of poetry, in "Pocket poem #1":

> I'm sure the world is tired
> of angry Black man poems
> about the struggle as much
> as those angry Black men
> are tired of struggling (p. 33)

These are not the poems of an "angry Black man;" nevertheless, they are poems from a Black man's perspective. When vasser-elong writes about "the struggle," rather than anger and directness his approach tends to be understated, subtle and oblique.

"Watching Monsters with Dad" p. 56, for instance, describes watching horror movies with his father, specifically the scene in *Frankenstein* in which the villagers chase the monster with fire and pitchforks. The poem concludes, "The black and white of the screen / set this motif in the distant past, / a relic of how people used to be." "The "black and white" of the scene subtly cues us to the ironic contemporary reference of the final line. The monsters are the villagers, *i.e.*, white folks, and not their target, the hated and feared "Other." It is a moment of epiphany shared by father and son.

In a similar understated vein, the poem "Vasser" p. 16, describes meeting white people who recognize his name as Dutch, and offer to connect him with his namesakes to see if they are related: "I can only imagine/that we are," he responds, "but not in the way that stimulates/a cheerful conversation." In "Reason" p. 9, he elaborates on name: "My name/knew/and where I lived/but not/who I was/or where I was/from." The name reveals where his ancestors were enslaved, not where they came from. It offers little clue as to vasser-elong's true identity.

"Vasser" alludes to the Dutch involvement in the slave trade that brought his ancestors to the Americas. And while contemporary racism underlies many of the poems in shrimp, vasser-elong's relationship to his African ancestry makes up the book's dominant theme. "My soul looks over the waters/carrying the weight of centuries" he writes in "In My Prayers," p. 10. The title shrimp refers to the author's diminutive height, which links him imaginatively to his Camaroonian ancestors. It also casts him doubly as an outsider: as a black man in America, and as a small man, a shrimp in a world populated by whales, And while "Life as a shrimp can be quite lonely," the struggle to forge an identity true to oneself in the face of misperceptions and stereotypes applied to African Americans dominates these poems. The problem is "to otherwise be you/when they see someone else" vasser-elong writes in "Nkyinkyini {Oon–chim-chim}" p. 69, a tribute to the vaudeville star Bert Williams.

vasser-elong sees images of Africanness, all around him in his neighborhood—for example, in the regal bearing of a lady walking to the laundromat carrying her basket on her head "as some women an ocean away,/also tote bags for miles in the sun." Despite his preoccupation with Africa, he complains in "King of the Jungle" p. 111, "the moment I confess that I am African/there is an explanation as to why I am not." And in fact, vasser-elong confesses in several poems that he's never been to Africa. His Africa is based on a combination of learning and yearning. The poems seem to yearn for a place, an Africa, free of the false identities America imposes on black men. An America where the best one can hope for is "the elegance of a well-lit cage." The basic problem many of the poems grapple with comes down to, "They say liberty lives in Africa / & yet this is where we are."

Variations on the identity issue are found in poems throughout the book. "Foster" p. 42, describes the adopted child "Tia who is now Ashley / raised in a family that looks nothing like what she sees / in the mirror, while straightening her hair." The poem asks, "What happens when she begins to question? ... When will she meet Alex Haley?" Here vasser-elong suggests the looming identity crisis of a young woman beginning to become self-aware.

Not all the poems are concerned with Africa or identity. "Junebug in the Alley" p. 69, strikes an optimistic note. It describes young boys in the hood, as "Olympians in training," as they leap over "mattresses / discarded from high rises." They seem to fly, "the open air at their feet." They are free in those moments. "Imagine what they see in themselves / as they run then leap," the poem asks. Only good things seem possible as they jump, "in pure confidence, / that they will make it over."

"Look" p. 75, on the other hand, begins less hopefully, advising us to keep both eyes open to be able to "see the world as it really is in its ugliest." But the poem concludes on a more positive note asking: "If one isn't willing to work in the dirt / then how can you really smell the flowers?"

And what better recommendation is there for a poet? jason vasser-elong is one who is willing to dig deeply into the dirt of his environment or the depths of his own consciousness. He leaves it to us to smell the flowers. ☒

—Michael Castro
poet and translator,
first Poet Laureate of St. Louis, 2017

Portrait

Paint me—oil on canvas
with my face
orange on one side
my eyes,
brown windows,
my nose full like the elephant
in the room;

paint my lips
in the smoothest of strokes
in fact, try to do it in two
indigo blues.

They say you live the blues,
my whole life a song
sung in the dusky basement
on an old stage,
one singer accompanied by
a pianist and a trumpeter—

have her sing it from the soul,
make those who listen
carry the weight of a lover
with his heart on his sleeve;

paint me — in the middle
of a room on a stool,
with water all around me
filling my bowl with life,
make it look like
the water is moving —
alive.

Reason

my name

knew

where i lived

i

but not

who i was

or where

i was

from.

In my prayers

i wonder how my incantations
fall on their ears.
If they can hear me and not who
has fashioned my tongue.

My soul looks over the waters
carrying the weight of centuries as

sharks
follow the trail
of our currency;
the questioning
of one's worth

        like pennies in the hand.

Heirloom

& so life begins in the middle,
for me, it was a ton of bricks
on the sunny streets of Saint Louis,

walking Delmar back
to the car my grandmother deeded
while she, in her eternal giving,
feeds flowers in a cemetery—
i still have yet to visit.

She is not there, but the gesture
is to pay respect, show homage
I will get there one day. Life found me

surrounded by moths, a candle
attracted to the other side   of death
as it moves and it moves and it moves
like time on my father's watch,

the Gucci he took his last breath in,
looking at the time,
          i am reminded
                    that it is limited.

The truest lie

This is the truest lie
shadow without a sun
light without a moon

and if i were ten again
it would matter to me,

that belt drawer would puuuull
the very melody of my heart strings,

but i have no tree on my back
or blistered finger tips —
only principal
only cause

i lie ever day in my blue jeans
oxford collared shirts —
i curse every time i open my mouth.

jason vasser-elong

Immigrant

It is the little things.
Someone told me once
that I was not African
because I hadn't grown up
in a village,

like a carrot
they dangled that fact
right in front of my face—

raaaacccccce, the briar rabbit
of our time;

i replied
in perfect diction:

well then, how does one
explain that I am not from
England either?

African

My past and present

Ancestral:

the mask looking back at me
from the mirror

jason vasser-elong

Wind/Quiet/Black

the sea is much larger
than i remember coloring as a child,
learning about maps, the world.

To be face to surface
             feels like a dream
without ever a thought of land
but endless water/water
bluer then i have ever seen —
                 and at night
the stars are flames in cast iron,
they are the beady eyes of my ancestors
that watch over the ocean,

its water cleaning their bones
rattling in the silence when i am alone
& my name tastes different on my tongue.

Vasser

is Dutch for vase
or German for water,
so white people tell me
when they shake my hand,
after we introduce ourselves.

They make a point
to educate me,
and immediately express
how they seldom meet
people like me with that name

and that I have a strong grip
before they list
the other Vassers they know,
questioning if we are related —

i can only imagine
that we are, but not
in the way that stimulates
a cheerful conversation.

jason vasser-elong

Poem at 38

Today, i saw a black man,
couldn't have been more than
            twenty-four seasons
into the rain of life —

he had on a Planet Sub t-shirt
and was with another black man
in thick locks wrapped like
            the nomads that ride camels along the Sahara.

He carried a make shift walking stick,
a large branch really, also wrapped
at what would be its handle.

For too long it seemed,
they would pace then sit,
pace then sit.

The young man,
recently off from the morning shift,
& the nomad were talking

when he all of a sudden

got up from his chair,
walked towards the parking lot
then proceeded to do twelve push ups
from the sidewalk—

customers parking their cars,
children looking on
pointing
then at me,
also a black man,
opening his book to read.

In homage

Along the coastline
the sand natural
against my naked feet,

i overlook the sunset,
sit and watch the sea gulls
fly over God knows —

buried years beneath
where i am distracted.

This is the same sun
that set on this same water
baptized with life,

given back to the Lord
before man could take
it away.

Sankofa

Blue feet browning
sand, trees, the smell of air
the sound of birds   again

she looks back over her tomb
then back into the trees
trembling to the shore.

jason vasser-elong

Character

Some days, i would study my mother
watch how she smiled—

even when i knew, she was hurting.
        Somehow, her eyes would
crescent moon, her mood steady

like beets on a plate, cantaloupe
in the fridge;
        her kids oblivious
that the Apple Circles were not
Apple Jacks, nor that

we did not have,
        because we always had
what we needed.

Sea Lion

Bearded self—
adrift

sheet of ice carries away

from known to unknown

A day in the life

for Shane

If God wears a beard, then so shall i—
tried to line, trim, until ultimately I cut the thing
right off my face, it peeled like tape
from a slick surface.

i read about him,
wondering if its she who really hears my prayers,
faithfully believing in the someday,

when someone will return—to walk in the light
and reach out for my sins
to breathe them in
like smoke from a pipe,

or fumes from
the Cadillac's that pass me—while i walk
the sidewalk alone
on my way from the dark to more dark.

So much for resembling my heavenly father—
or is it my heavenly mother from whom i get my eyes?

And my skin is not white, nor fair, but brown
like the paper bag, that covers the bottles,

like those that line the sidewalk, drink from,
that watch,

and my hair is nappy when it grows
like weeds in the summer,
rarely hangs below my neck line
or blows in the wind.   It mostly sits there

like ghettos in big cities
motionless and tightly knit
waiting for a comb.

September 15, 2017

Today they let another blue life
take another black one

back, back to Birmingham in the sixties
back to the East Saint Louis of 1917
back to some plantation

somewhere, anywhere, Missouri?

i suppose there is no room for black
on the American flag,

no room to acknowledge,
to show pride for the backbone
there is no solace
for the weary,

no room to let their hands free
that are consumed by the monster
left to toil around
in the squalor
of their forgotten dreams
of promise.

They say liberty lives in Africa
& yet *this* is where we are.

Gemini woman

Hardened with time soft
in the contours of line,

i once admired a paper mache
sculpture of a Gemini woman;

Liberty and Liberia
soil connected life reflected
in the black and white of life.

Bachelor of arts

I wonder where in the world i can earn a degree
in Ghomala?

Learn the history of important names and dates
        the events that led to this or that revolution

therefore, i may preserve and protect the sacred teach-
ings —
                study its prose and poetry,

where looking for meaning it too will read, as in English
                of or pertaining to origin,

but where the language is not straightforward
but vastly coarse as is the texture
        of the hair   on the people   where it is used.

Ethnographic Study:
short people in a circle

Every once in a while
you will find a group
of short people
in a circle talking about
the fires that have burned
down their tiny houses,

how the smoke
filled their little lungs
with dollops of gray smoke,
and their miniature pinschers
have gone without pro plan
for breeds ten pounds and under.

they cry little bitty tears
that are so small
they could barely
qualify as tears at all,

rather an idea,

jason vasser-elong

that their lives
are always like this,
that they live
for booster seats
and ladders litter
their living rooms
filled with small portraits
and little flat screen tv's

and of course
they are descendants
of pygmies
that lived under leaves
in little jungles
in itsy bitsy countries

where they drive
tiny cars
that can be picked up
with one hand,

where even when
they stand, they are
barely even seen
everything of theirs is small,
they have little dreams
and baby nightmares
and wake up to tiny screams
but no one can hear them
because they are so tiny,
and cute and are novelties
and their names are

abbreviated with adjectives
like *little* before i

or given superlatives
like *lil bit* &
they pay

little bills
and have little thrills
in small cities
where they live,
nearly hidden,
and where they
are seldom if not,
almost always overlooked.

Introducing Mason Bassett

for Olaudah Equiano also known as Gustavus Vassa

He grabbed the face towel
to remove the black
until the skin pared pink
across the surface.

Ignoring the whispers
became rooms without doors,
windows or light. For him,
daylight was a lamp
and night was the sun.

Remnants of his past
stained the white towel
and never left the fiber—
destined

like the exodus
that led to questioning
the currency of one's weight
in cowries,
iron bars or rum.

& sugar no longer sweetens

and drinking coffee
becomes a ritual
needed in the waking hours
when the Windsor meets the center,
and oxfords carry his stride.

Dog people

It comes back around
ignoring /what cannot be/ ignored

because some things will not
change. Say a cat, that is
always teased
around spools of yarn,

nip, and those—that
for no other reason
just do not like cats,
especially those
that find themselves
unlucky or under ladders.

Pocket poem #1

I'm sure the world is tired
of angry Black man poems
about the struggle / as much
as those angry Black men
are tired of struggling

Song for spring

i would like it to be routine
but these pages glaring back
intimidate with a blank stare

i date the margin
assign an age to something
much older than me
then name it, forever changing its face

adding then adding more —
scratching out my mistakes
on an otherwise perfect sleeve of paper
that has probably been recycled
from the jungle.

Maybe a Macaque climbed its tree,
ate its fruit then slept
before its silent collapse
to the grass by a human hand,

hopefully it died
falling in the breeze
of those still standing,
their leaves   playing the melody
all trees hear near their end

branches caressed in the warmth
and cool spray of light,

jason vasser-elong

ecstasy of heavy rain
passionate thunder—

maybe there is life
in its remains,
that there are flowers
in the cavities of bark
wilted and soft

its twisted frame
a sculpture
the story of its life
a poem.

Operation maroon

When one jumped
we all moved—

like a unit of little army men
whose mission was to take down
whomever we had to, for the family;

cuz we were brothers to my sister,

all of our mothers
with apples on their desks,

our fathers all cool.

The summer takes me back
before high school
& i can remember running
from house to house to stay up late
and play,

i can remember when one
got a whipping
we all had to,

we were a tribe of Js,
knee deep in video games,
Barbie dolls and house parties

jason vasser-elong

bumping around through life
in our roller skates & tap shoes.

Who knew those years would fade
like the sides
of our heads?

Gutter rainbow

for Talib Kweli

Sometimes God cries, and
tears are left in the gutters
attached to housing projects

where a child colors
within the lines of an instruction booklet
with a broken crayon,
near a garden littered with weeds —

but when it rains, God's tears form a rainbow
in that gutter / which leads
to a flower bed,
that blossoms in new light.

Somewhere, there is a leaf in the world
looking for its tree

      finding home away from its forest.

jason vasser-elong

Subtraction

Today, I sit with
who i have become,
waiting for the blood
to be cleaned from re -
sponsible hands that stand
where it all happened —

before concrete & city
streets, before the clocks
held on to bricks, their hands
moving as the sun moves,
where before these trees
were planted, other trees grew.

Thinking of *Today's Math*, &
Bonair-Agard's Trinidad,
wondering about my own
response, my own manner
of moving across time, &
i'm left with looking into
a mirror, at the face of what
it looks like — years after trees
have been dug up, after
new ones have been planted.

Arthropod

I is the memory of one's self
and *me* is the experience of i;
so in the abstract, it is the confluence
of rivers that lead to my ocean
where there is perspective,
searching for life,
protecting the vision.

I cannot remember
when i learned that when among giants
i would have to be the bigger person,
to somehow divert the seemingly whimsical—
from my beating fist of a heart,
expecting to react instead
i redirected, retreated to the dark.

Life as a shrimp can be quite lonely,
but every once in a while
i would see other shrimp make their way about
The decayed, picking up pieces of the past
only to make use of its history, and it is in those
moments that makes for pleasant swimming
among blue whales, almost as if i too
am heavy, significant,
that i am a wonder to behold.

The accident

Tumbling down Pernod Avenue, a white car sped danger-ously towards the hospital; a woman in labor about to bring a baby girl into a cold world on a hot day in August. With-out room to maneuver, the car smashed into other cars, not just mine, on its descent down a mountainous city street in the wee hours of a Tuesday morning. Before the light of day, while those working at a neighborhood café tied their aprons around tired hips that had yet to feel the thrill of a day's work, their legs balanced on already tired feet.

He forgot to turn his head lights on, but managed to stop at the stop sign, his tires skidding; leaving black war wounds next to my driver's side mirror, broken into pieces of a dream that i wished it was, when i discovered the debris. No note, no apology, just the cry of a baby coming into a reckless world, almost sure of leaving her to question why.

Foster

for Tia and her kin

What happens when they begin to question?
Their reflections pointing to the obvious —
or when they are taken and given names
by the eager to save?

Just who will they become
when they face themselves
for the first time away from the nest,
on the ground where lurking,
searching for their truth in a place —
hides the subliminal, and they become afraid
of what they see.

Who teaches dem to comb their kitchens?
or how to speak so their messages are felt
by those willing to teach the insignificance
of gold teeth or that nappy is not a bad thing
but part of who they really are?

When will they meet Alex Haley?
and how will you explain that Kunta was never Toby;
yet she used to be Tia, who is now Ashley,
raised in a family that looks nothing like what she sees
in the mirror, while straightening her hair.

jason vasser-elong

Probability

i guess one *could* say that aliens
built the pyramids

moved bricks of sand
with their minds,

left their mark on the walls
so that in time the world would know
it was *alien genius* that moved stones

the size of rooms in noon blistering
sunshine.

Suppose it was alien labor
of a different kind

that built the Americas
as their alien ancestors crafted Giza
from the world around them,

perhaps there are aliens among us
right now, listening to our secrets,
cooking our food,

raising our babies with their foreign hands
and watchful eyes on the stars aligned
that guided them here,

then again, Negro was synonymous
with alien, so i guess you're right.

AfriKen doll

For Sal

Behold
a machine
designed to make a man
packaged—with detachable feet

his many hats.

His country of origin is yours to name—
        with different sizes of chains to contain
complete with an Afro, and an assortment of interchange-
able tees,
jeans,   dashikis and Barbie's

sold separately for you to dream
        then act out your inner most fantasies
of making more

go on explore
        position him

make him yours.

Stand him   only   to break him
        back to black and plastic
after use

sell him on Amazon
        realistic and complete with hang ups
        & full inches of authentic

bendable   moldable   man

that will bounce when thrown

        smiling back at you from the ground.

Bell peppers

Every once in a while
a good meal is all one needs,
to take off the day
& put on a memory –

fastened with the way she smiled
as you two picked
the right bell peppers,
red and yellow,

how she touched your hand
as you glanced,
reading her lips *thank God*
at your presence,

you looking at
what cut of chicken
would fare well with bell
peppers, each one
complementing the other.

jason vasser-elong

Rooted

an ekphrastic poem after Carol Shinn's Beyond the Tree

From here
even the grass
looks tall
peppering the base
of an old tree
that has probably
seen it all,

its branches
stretching across
a forest,

its roots exposed,
protruding
from its soil & moss
finches walk across
then rest on twigs,

they are so small
you can only
hear them sing.

Finches

i remember learning that they were finches,
from Zambia,
and it dawned on me

that though they had wings,
they couldn't clear the walls that kept them

hopping from perch to corner/corner to perch—
i was ten.

Had yet to understand
the importance of place

but i knew they wanted to fly
or at least hop around the ground,
feel blades of grass, build nests
hunt for whatever their little bird hearts desired.

i surmise many of us are raised like that

trying with allllll of our might
to just be birds,

feel the open air under our bellies
to be raised within the leaves
of our own choosing

jason vasser-elong

The city is like that
a jungle, and behold all of the birds
looking up at the sky   as they walk.

beneath my skin are feathers,
what comes out as words are really songs
and i have to thank all of those that flew before

so that i may know the elegance
of a well-lit cage.

Envy

The leaves blow
here and there
in their own time
Deciduous Maples,
being who they want
riding the wind
sun at their backs
stems point like arrows
falling from steep rock bluffs
pointing here and there
being who they want
riding the wind
everywhere they are
among the changing
weightless many
they graze conifers
on their way
riding the wind
being who they want
stems pointed like arrows
falling from steep rock bluffs
watching from the inside
through a window
watching from the inside
through a windshield
they ride the wind
be who they want
in their own time
they sway to the winds

50   jason vasser-elong

of change and rest
atop the grass
other leaves
buildings, everything
until they blow
here and there
the sun at their backs.

Fields of Marigold

for Aunt Val

Fields of Marigold
glistening one October morning
remain when the sun has gone away,
they dance on the wind
to songs strummed by angels
on red harps

right there,
where the clouds part
to meet the blue
just   above   the   trees.

If you look up
there is a song
that will catch you listening,
a laugh lingering
in the leaves of autumn
fall and crackle as they
orange then brown;

there is wisdom in their aging
comfort that they will
come around season after
season after the rain
& heat of summer.

jason vasser-elong

You can count on the leaves
to change you're somber
to joy in the cool crisp
of morning when God
paints the sky,
when ducks
take to the pond.

Two ducks

My arms wrapped around
locked   and her heartbeat
a melody into my chest.

Two ducks greeted me,
they had just left the pond
the sun shimmering their wet feathers,

for a moment, i felt my own heart—
as if for the first time.

Mixed

for Jada

My sister used to switch
the head of her black Barbie
with that of the white one;

that was what mixed meant
to a young light skinned girl
growing up in the eighties,

playing with the possibility
that it could be that simple.

She would sit for hours and play
with the both of them
driving around the basement
in the pink corvette convertible
it too having lost its head,

& the two of them would
be pushed along the black
and white checkered tile

to watch The Junk Yard Dog
and Big John Stud
wrestle it out for an imaginary
title that neither one of them
would win.

Watching monsters with Dad

My father and i
watched classic monster movies,

i would swing my legs from the couch
and watch Frankenstein be chased
by people with pitchforks and fire.

The black and white of the screen
set this motif in the distant past,
a relic of how people used to be.

jason vasser-elong

Creature

That's the thing about him,
       soil from his home country lining the coffin,
where he dreams the day away until night
only to rise again and take   life

the liquid that carries the history of families
       are rivers, rolling rivers
and it's funny because running water will send him back
       how beautiful the irony—

the sun must have never looked so beautiful
as if seen for the last time

retreating behind clouds
high in the mountains, nestled behind trees.

i too had turned my back on the cross
not God, for there were gods before they came to correct

       but unlike the prince of darkness i can look at the sun
and admire that it was there
and i can remember what it feels like on my skin
almost as if the soil of my home country was a blanket
almost as if i lived in a cold—cold world.

Poem for Holland

i often lay awake awhile
obsessing about the past
and all of the time
between then and now
orange and black,

they call people like me,
over there, the afro dutch;
and suffice it to say
that part does not bother
me much, it is just, well —

we have to hyphenate
ourselves, divide our
bodies into two piles,
even our mouths
carry two tongues
and while
most are born with two legs,
where can we run to
and be one, one thing —

there is this sting
that i get inside my heart
when i think of your part
in the transatlantic
tragic secret, our children
learn about in outdated
books, how they can

jason vasser-elong

never understand
those years ago
their lives were
all part of some global
plan, their role
that of the slave,
the builder of worlds
the mothers of children
reduced to whispers that
never had a chance
at normalcy,

we still turn our heads
at the sight of mixed
babies born from white
and black parents that
may truly love each other
but because of your brothers
your sisters, your fathers
& your mothers, we have classes
about "diversity" and have
to take "deeper dives" into the
the curriculum; we sit
in concentric talking circles
and have arguments about religion
and culture and how language
is a barrier, and in truth

i admire your attempt
at atonement in your
day of remembrance
in May, and I'll agree

that it is a start at change,

but i thought you would
want to know, that I think
of you in the way
that i surmise someone that
was raped, abused or
sodomized thinks of the
one or few that robbed
them of their innocence,
that held the wool over
their eyes.

jason vasser-elong

Seven

Out of an eternal desert Far East
the most sacred of stones was lost -
to winds strong and heavy and swift,
for temple nor grave have saved hence,
the sound of its hollow against walls
filled with the wisdom of ages past
was found buried in Ithaca one winter.

Negro:

Ancestral line

caught in the
        middle

of westward — expansion.

A Jewel

for those Sphinxmen in Ithaca, New York: 1906

Stirred fellows forming
African refugee society –
Shining.

Laundry day in the city

She was regal
on her way to the Laundromat
bag on her head,
one under her arm,
a purse.

With the ease of wearing a hat
she made her way
as some women an ocean away
also tote bags for miles in the sun.

i *too* have known rivers

i too have known rivers,
that carry memories beneath
to where they began,

filling the shell with whispers
of the past.

i have known some to have bridges
that provide passage
from land to land,
hand to hand,
voice to voice,
heart to heart.

i believe their masters
seek passage across
to where the future is
as certain as suspension
carrying the years in her bosom.

On becoming men

For Jamar

Remember Mickey D's in the summers after track?
   It was 1989:

before my parents divorced, before your pops got sick,
   back then

we ran in heats, our young Pumas would barely
   touch the lane

running running too fast to see the end coming
   to all we understood

about being boys and becoming men.

jason vasser-elong

Fear of heights

Children don't expect the world
to chew them up,

all they know is how to run
after wild animals,

wanting to touch and to feel
everything they can,

imagine how it felt to walk
for the first time,

to not know what falling was
and yet you got up
to have at it again.

When I ran around my mother's carpet
in a blue onesie,
i shocked myself going after a ball

snapped and popped
but didn't stop   trying—

it wasn't until I became a man
that i acquired a fear of heights.

The father

After The Mother by Gwendolyn Brooks

i never knew your names
or saw your faces

but i saw as your shoes hung
from the telephone wires
juxtaposed the high rises,
along the street corners, knowing

that somehow that was a sign,
that you tried to reach me
so you left your message.

jason vasser-elong

Junebug in the alley

In the hood,
there are Olympians in training

flipping from the concrete slabs
in alley ways with perfect form

springing from mattresses
discarded from the high rises.

Imagine what they see in themselves
as they run then leap—

the open air at their feet
in pure confidence,

that they will make it over.

Men talking

From deh east
side of the street
in baggy jeans — heavy left leg,
he walks.

From the west
side of the street
buttoned up and sure,
he walks.

Both approach an awning
the one in the baggy jeans nods up
the buttoned up one nods down

without a single word

so much was said.

jason vasser-elong

Eraser

After Grass by Carl Sandburg

I used to hold within my blades,
under my soil   the proof

but they dug it up
and replaced me with asphalt,
concrete, and with stop signs
and mile markers, speed limits,
& city limits —

but I am still the grass beneath the streets,
hiding those blood stained memories with
places to go and people to see.

44 West

There is an ocean of asphalt on either side,
riding along from the base of fields
headed somewhere, dodging schools of sea horse,
sharks speeding by headed for prey –
         i caught the wind of a Mayflower
on its way,

as was commonplace
when highways were waterways

some things remain —

but look in the rock cliffs,
where the silt holds history
encased in stone, where geographic
hieroglyphs tell of a past;

whales pass in both directions,
carrying the mass,

along the rivers
children are drowning,
left on the side of the road
as the world just moves along
like tide out to sea.

jason vasser-elong

Remnant

Beneath deh shores of Granada
you live in stone configured
as you would have been, had you lived.

As a descendant of one that survived
i pray you peace beneath the heavy water—
under the weight of history
waiting to be discovered
for the questions to arise.

Beneath the shores
adjacent to sunken ships and the bones
of your former selves— you are beautiful,
in your defiance to the depths
to the mouths of sharks,

grazing the backs of whales curious as to why
you are not finned.

shrimp

Blue

For Tonya

Maybe they were swimming
or floating in the air,
i cannot recall,

but i remember you there
amidst so many
your frame, the outline of your hair

how it moved
when you turned your head
almost in rhythm as i reached
palms facing up
you floating down to me
so close
that i could have broken your shadow;

in fact i did
and you disappeared
right before my eyes.

i remember
the way your locks,
flowed like ribbons in slow motion
out into the air

or in to the ocean
where i jumped
where i swam
and overcame my deepest fears.

jason vasser-elong

Look

it isn't enough to live
with one eye open, the other winced,
you must open both—
        see the world as it really is in its ugliest,

without her makeup on,
before she has had her coffee.

You have to understand the context
of her argument with the sun this morning,
how hot she got.

If one isn't willing to work in the dirt,
        then how can you really smell the flowers.

American:

My present and past

lineage:

the mask looking back at me
from the mirror.

Middle ground

For no other reason than curiosity
i stepped to a man
walking west on Delmar Boulevard
in a confederate flag ball cap

and asked what it meant to him,
his reply bellied pride from the south,
that he had black friends,
and that we might as well
take down the American Flag;

i thought about that

as we walked east
trying to find middle ground
amidst the construction.

i will go to Meshuggah's

for a cup of coffee —
& stare at the street lights
or watch the people
stroll pass the windows
let time have its way.

i'll drift off and listen
to the creek of the door
as people stumble in
surveying for a space
to place their books
open their writing pads.

i was drawn to this woman
leisurely strolling the sidewalk,
her baby girl
bundled and slung across
her chest in blue cloth,
resting against her chest —

her pink berets shook
as her mother's feet
travelled above the stars.

Delmar Loop pantoum

Never a good sign,
folks pointing, looking around
a mob forms, cars slow
they stop.

Folks pointing looking around
i leave the café to watch,
they stop.
looking at them like the others,

i leave the café to watch
among the rest of us,
and look at them like the others
other poets, artists, the Avant - garde.

Among the rest of us
in tune, inspired
other poets, artists, the Avant- garde
all of us are aware,

inspired
by all the colors,
other poets, artists, the Avant- garde,
we all desire

in tune, we are inspired
admiring the likeness of Chuck Berry
desiring,
man on the corner panhandles.

shrimp

We admire the likeness of Chuck Berry,
a mob forms, cars slow
man on the corner panhandles
never a good sign.

Nichols island

From the photographs,
Nichols Island
looks like a mountain
emerging from the ocean,
beyond the coast line,

isolated

as Mary's parents must have felt
watching the earth shatter
beneath them,

how the water swelled
flooding their dreams
sealing their wounds in salt.

Acculturation

he was pops back then,
who played loud white people's music, as i called it.

i was confused by him whistling and shuffling cards
        to the beat of what I've never listened to
    long enough to relate to;
but he was himself,

something i then had yet to find
        in my dreadlocks that stretched to my behind
        and a chip on my shoulder / dat weighed heavy on
my mind

there was freeedom in his ridiculous

                something authentic

like old shoes repaired
then worn again.

Loafers

One day those shoes will be filled,
a toddler will crawl in them

stumble, fast enough to run
and the propulsion will send them

learning how to strut
then eventually walk

like someone old enough
to buy new ones.

Shake

For Dad

i knew my father was dead
when i saw his hands,
never mind the gray i never saw

those two re-appear like a face i once knew,
askew   old and wrinkled   barely holding four aces.

i understood he was gone
from the placement of those four

my grandmother was there
and she said " that's not Butch, he isn't smiling"

I smile when i remember
when i look in the mirror
or when my mother complains that i look just like him

so i shaved my beard
showing the world my dimpled chin that i never liked

hoping he will still recognize me
from above.

Ujamma

Right now
i'm writing on top of an ant colony,

they find my pages
and i notice one discover
the pool of water left from my glass —

in small mounds
they amass and cover,

brave little ones
working around me
as if i am not even there.

Nkyinkyini {*O* on-chim-chim}

For Bert Williams

You were somebody
to a pair of wide eyes under mahogany skin
      shining from the rafters
                    or the floor of the balcony
but you never looked up,

they never saw the pain behind your curtain
nor the ways that your skin matched theirs in the light,

or that your darkness was blacker than a thousand midnights
over the Atlantic,

where the stars also look down from above.

jason vasser-elong

At dinner

i ate myself;
enjoyed smoked gouda
& red grapes, groundnuts
from home, i dined
on fu fu chicken stew

and one of Dad's ribs,
plantains, hot water
cornbread, some fried fish.

i drank some Tempranillo,
& had paella as a side, even

tried to make my mom's
salmon croquets
with a dash of Thyme
some collards, corn,
kidney beans and swai,
& i really can't complain —

because i finished it all off
with a little slice of Gran's
lemon meringue.

Black face

i read about the Black Arts Movement
even shook Baraka's hand after we talked
about the unity and the struggle.

Back in his day, many of us shed our slave names
for blacker ones like Muhammad or Amiri—
imagine that, all of these people
walking the streets of their birth—New Jersey, Kentucky
or St. Louis with names blacker than asphalt,

while back in my ancestral home,
our President's name is Paul and deh youth
in rural country sides / they nod their heads to Biggie
and Pac; while I tune in to Makossa
and nod my own.

Elong {eh-Long}

For those first twenty
traded for food in Virginia,

for the Argonauts and their voyage—
my golden fleece was a phoenix
in September, two thousand fourteen

for my mother's mother mother
who lived among the breeze
and the wind knew my name,

for when the stars became my friends
that twinkled when they saw big momma's
momma run to the north and her kin across the water,
who cried from the coastline to the ghosts in my ears,
for those at Fernando Po,

for my nephews who need to know who they are.

Falling in Love

When you fall in love
it's only natural you'll get hurt,
there is beauty in allowing
just that—

the sting, cutting
through years of longing

like a paper cut
it's there
waiting for air—
for you to notice

that to love
is to bleed
for someone else.

jason vasser-elong

Rules for rain

Fall
deliberately
lightly
to soothe,

fall
hard
to cleanse
wipe away
amend
send litter to the sewer
blood from granite
tears from faces,

fall
like a wave
from the ocean
topple
splash
erase   hate

send salt from cars,

fall
on strangers leaving bars
so they may cleave,
leave clouds
always fall   down
atop the heads

clearing
washing
releasing
the heat of the day,

for flowers
gardens
the forest at bay,
for trees to grow
and produce
for grass to grow
and produce,

for love tastes like rain
smells like rain
feels like rain on the skin
waiting to be cleansed
to be wanted
caressed
and felt—
to bring more life
or just to try

love,

fall
deliberately
over
to run down
to help
newer love
stay new

92

old love too

just fall

just fall

just

fall.

Daydream

The rain made him daydream that they were away some-
place, away from work, away from the familiar. Perhaps
the two of them had found themselves holding hands while
walking along a path of some ancient city, away from the
tourists, on a quiet boulevard with cobble stoned streets and
storefronts that have been around for centuries. There, they
are noticed but not observed, are spoken to and smiled
upon in the way that smiling transcends any language, the
understanding of human care and acceptance that they
felt as they passed others on their way. Some also holding
hands, others not. It was the kind of place where the flowers
smiled back at you. All of the beautiful colors of the build-
ings, their moldings and the ornate windows adorned in
silks and tapestry hand woven with time, which had. Time to explore together.

Leisurely walking, making eye contact, the casionally stop, allow the wind and the qu
bodies, to fill the void, and then slowly one
the other and the pillows of their lips would
they laid in one another's arms, swaying b
if in a slow dance to the music of their love would
be heard would be a bird chirping off into the distance and
the sound of their breath and the delicate touches of lips that
have waited far too long to meet. Sun fading into a darken-
ing sky, already brushed with pink clouds in the sleepy haze
of twilight, they'd stroll the curving silhouettes of corners that
have known lovers before. They'd pass initials carved into
the sides of old homes, an art gallery, which she noticed had

a large candy red vase illuminating under florescent, and then they'd be greeted with the smell of fresh bread as they came upon a café.

She stole a peck and playfully took off running, her sundress flowing in the summer breeze, taunting him with "come and get me" as she looked back into hungry eyes. Stumbling then catching his balance, he starts after her, his right hand reaching for her, and he catches her, like a fly in a web, and holds her close to his beating heart, her panting breath, their bodies against the café, pressed together, and rain found them there unmoved, a fixture seeming to have always been there.

A twinkle in the eye

i grew
into my name
in the way that
someone learns
to prepare
hot water cornbread
in a cast iron skillet,

how the white corn
is made brown
when you add
 a little bit of this
and a little bit of that,
with your hands

you must mold
and shape it
how it should be
before gently
setting heat
to its sides.

jason vasser-elong

The other zoo

for Hugo, the other Alpha at the Saint Louis Zoo

There is a reason the Chimpanzees
all walked towards us
one by one —

standing at the window to their world.

Amassed, they turned and watched too
in the direction that we pointed and awed;

a child knocked on the glass, an ape turned
knocked back,

then stared past the child's young eyes;
and while the child began to cry from fear

Hugo grinned and with his hands
he covered his ears.

The way that i am

Running with knives,
my heart on my sleeve,
trusting, the way a stranger
falls back blindly into
a fellow stranger's arms;

i believe, then
i believe again.

jason vasser-elong

Gravitational

pull of the eyes
to the open sky

so there / it's almost not

there is only breath
and the soul.

The stars are only burning
only living
they are candles
while we seek purple.

To feel is to live
the secret life of flowers

bees the great thinkers
of our time,

how else can one explain
the dance of lovers?

So still that they move.

Devil at the enchanted jungle

It's the little things,
that move me,

i was called a little monkey
when only a child
by someone evil, with wild eyes
walking the crosswalk before he spat
on my mother's windshield,

and i remember my mom
breaking two glass bottles
defending my honor.

Just recently while at the zoo,
i walked to view the chimpanzees
and from a cluster some old devil
mentioned me—in the context of the animals
and said it twice.

It's hard to pretend
as i have only two cheeks to turn
and yet in every direction there is evil—
but i refuse to look down
but into the beady eyes of the devil
who turns away from my face.

A-Z

a: to adolescence with questions that will get answered in adulthood.

b: to behave like your name suggests, to be...

c: to care.

d: to demand the respect from a world that takes and takes and takes.

e: to expect nothing less, because you give nothing more.

f: to forgive, to forgive, to forgive.

g: to give.

h: to have love, my father said once that you don't see love, but you see the results of love.

i: to identify, by looking in the mirror and recognize the beauty in your brokenness.

j: to justify why you are, who you are, when you are, to whomever asks.

k: to be kind.

l: to live with the choices you have made, but to not let those choices define.

m: to move without haste.

n: to never deny your worth in the presence of the rich.

o: to otherwise be you when they see someone else.

p: to pray even when you don't think God is listening.

q: to question, always question, question everything.

r: to release is to let go of the past, in order to relish the present.

s: to save yourself for what's most important.

t: to take nothing for granted.

u: to seek understanding, my grandfather would say that "to understand, is to seek understanding."

v: to venerate your culture and the culture of those you meet in the streets, on a subway, café, on the bus, to trust that to love your own self is to show love to others.

w: to be willing to stand on principle; if you stand for something—you won't fall for anything.

x: to xylophone (just kidding) to never be xenophobic, which means to have fear or hatred for strangers or foreigners.

y: to yearn for it is not enough, you must go after it.

z: to Zebra when you find yourself in a barn.

Unicorn / an ars poetica

A *Negro Love Song* in the pocket
of a pair of corduroy, it was an orange sky
& i could tell because the trees,

they were all mirrors, their leaves
seemed to all point toward the sun,
looking down — its crown
of porcupine quills & bright eyes

& shadows danced around the playground,
which i chased in mix match shoes,
one red the other blue, in a t-shirt
that told the whole world
who i belonged to if lost
or stolen, but who would steal a child?
but the harsh reality, that would show up
in the closet or under the bed.

i jumped back — with a fist full of poems
in my head, ready & aimed,
becoming, becoming –
how quickly did they pirouette
like my sister's feet

how soon did they find me
under water, swimming upstream.

Lunar

With so many poems
about the moon

it's hard to angle verse
so that verbs move
when pulled by the muse

so galactic when full
so quiet it screams from the sky.

jason vasser-elong

Monster

Even a man who is pure at heart and says his prayers by
night ...may become a wolf when the wolfsbane blooms
and the autumn moon is bright. —Curt Siodmak

Just beneath the surface   whispering
          in all the words i hate—

moving in the shadows so only i can see.

It's in me
          watching from the inside
          painting the air with my voice

forcing a grin in revenge
          that nearly salivates
     when the victim becomes the victor.

i suppose i've always found comfort in the Wolf Man;
          lived in his nightmares
          became the animal within
          because its expected—you see

to be wild, to be angry in my happiest moments

live in squalor, to use a noose for a neck tie.

i might as well let him loose
          cause one can only hang around so long
before the world begins to notice.

Lady bug

i feel your presence
right before you call or text—

at just the right moment
you are there
when i really want
to hear your laugh,

even now there is a lady bug
resting on my book
crawling in my direction.

jason vasser-elong

Ode to our hands

the hand that writes this
found purpose in yours
the warmth, how it tingles at its tip

earned kisses from you
trembling under the soft,
delicate stroke of your index
then middle, until finally your thumb strums

a melody our fingers dance to —
palm to palm

how the song sends my whole body
to sway like it's
a summer's day on a beach
in Michigan,

and for miles there is sand and water
and sunshine and laughter

as if for an instant,
we are physically there
somewhere away from anywhere we know

but our hands understand,
they felt around and found places to play
and we found ourselves in the middle

in the center of a room,
that for those moments became a place
we really wanted to be until
we opened our eyes to see that
paradise can be next to the fridge

and that heaven
can be as close
as the kitchen sink.

jason vasser-elong

Presence

A blanket and an open window
or ear and an embrace

listening to you is a song
without words—
a poem both rhymed and
unrhymed, a story
with no beginning and no end,

it is a dance timed by movement
music its gentle soliloquy,

and i wonder   how soon
it will be to be warm,

smell the fresh air
feel the breeze on my face
to hear you—to feel you

to speak without words
and think in poems,

to read about your life—
        from the doorstep of your eyes
to meander without reason
to sing even though i can't.

Move / Aspirant / Stand still

i wonder about those Othello
      teetering an impossible line
as their steps forgo their pasts.

At what demise is the successful one?
      what languages must be denied
to be understood?

For their very faces
to mirror the goal, for their reflections
to appear free,   for their toiled feet
to ignore the pain, for their path's destiny —

is to forget the shadow
      only to walk in the dreams of someone else

what of those fantasies of wild men

      living with animals and their women
discarded back to the jungle.

How then does one reconcile with Tarzan?

jason vasser-elong

King of the jungle

i don't know what to make of Tarzan,
as I type, its underlined red to capitalize his name,
      but *Elong* is nowhere in the dictionary.

i don't know what to make of Tarzan,
swinging from vine to vine, beating his chest
      and I surmise for the same reason
i am glad to have never been a Rhodes Scholar,

though i take the A train back and forth to Aethiopia,
back and forth through Ithaca,
back and forth to the Nile valley and Kemet
and the mastabas in the courtyard.

i don't know what to make of Tarzan,
      who would suspect that there is danger in a
screaming white man in the trees?

And the world accepts this motif,
accepts his apeish manner of knuckling the ground when
he walks
but i am the monkey, the signifying money
Jack Johnson, the first heavyweight champ of color
The Big Smoke who was made to be a giant Gorilla
Black Animal in the heart of New York City, A King Kong
or Homo giganthropithicus somewhere getting studied
in Tuskegee.

i don't know what to make of Tarzan
        i don't buy the brand of the English wearing the
mask of the African that can be removed
and then that same mask   my face   is the subject of
internet Bravado and minstrel
that i can only be black and American and hip hop and
jazz and pop and dancing around all cool like and smooth
and hip and eating chicken and drinking Hen
and the moment i confess that i am African,
there is an explanation as to why i am not.

i am put back in the box, back in the chicken yard
back in the plastic — how does one reconcile
how does one wrestle with being wild
how does one cope with value bestowed
like i am some actor in a play portraying the role   of
the primitive
while there is some white man in the jungle
or some white woman playing Cleopatra;

when will it be ok for me to swing from trees
to beat my chest and not get shot?

Drummer boy

for Dr. E.

He looks to the right
towards the East
at his elders,

In a kufi with a Djembe between his knees
keeping time.

He learns as we all do
by watching / by doing / readying himself
to one day lead.

Turtle power

for my Nephews

Who would think
that four brothers
from the bottom
could take on the world—

they amazed me too
and have for all these years,

those turtles helped me
to conquer my fears
of being different.

Sometimes, i feel green
like the world is looking at me
from behind an iron mask
shredding my insides,

but in those moments
i remember the sewer
and if those four could last
& take on the foot clan,
then so can i.

Visit

In the park, i watch birds
fly from their perch on bushes,
gutters—then somewhere between the fence line,

& out beyond

someone would call my name.

Cardinals mostly,
their red in constant contrast,

made me feel lucky—as if it were not a bird at all,
but a butterfly and before it died,

it had to let me know

that it lived.

Madeira island

In my dreams
sometimes i listen to Fado
in the harbor,

& overlook the hillside
of beautiful villas stacked as if

one could climb those terra cotta
steps to the highest peak
of Mount Pico—

those orange roofs of homes
lead to the clearest sky,

where you'd swear you could see
well into the past.

Along the beach,
my bare brown feet
invade the shoreline

as the proof of my being there
is around for only a moment
then it's taken out to sea.

jason vasser-elong

Keepsake

Who needs sleep
when there are dreams
revealing themselves
peeling back layer
after fragile layer
until only the core remains

to be broken like bread
and shared with the fondest
of memories already present
swimming in the ease of morning
calming waters, fields of green—

there isn't a blue so rich as the sky
when I look into your eyes   and i

find myself lost in your forest,
mesmerized in your endless limbs
that keep me as a spider keeps

wrapped around
spin a net with my heart, you
my black widow   take me
hold me in your embrace as a singer
holds a song   let rest find us
mixed together   woven

let's make baskets with our bodies
so that there will always be a place
to keep our hearts

Pocket poem #2

"But you've never been to Africa!"

Not yet, but you wouldn't expect
a Scottish terrier to have been
to Scotland, would you?

jason vasser-elong

Mangroves

There is a green
that blooms in the trees of the Cameroon
miles away from here, yet not so far   away;
imagining the shade of a fern in Bafoussam

or the bamboo there
where my soul has never forgotten
though my lungs have yet to breathe her air
imbibe her smells
hold her rich soil.

Stronger still is the memory
of the Mangroves that border
the Bamboo forest
that lead to my Atlantic.

My Atlantic

Is a rainforest in colors
vast as a great ocean,
a garden of creation
that becomes even more alive
at night, under a full moon —

each generation
building off the next,
sea fans, sponges kept in balance
by Parrot fish and Spanish dancers
sway to the current
in their red mantels —

trumpet fish use their muse
and become what they lay against
and decorator crabs,
in their thrift,
carry life, as do millions of beautiful
                              colorful fish
grooming themselves
against the backs of sharks.

jason vasser-elong

Wise bird Villanelle

What does the wind know anyway?
where on earth is my name?
Ubiquitous, watching from every which way

busy bees working for honey, we play
drinking the milk, playing the game
What does the wind know anyway?

seeing all — all the time — all day
i'm sure from all angles we look the same
Ubiquitous, watching from every which way

looking for direction or some way
to sankofa broken pieces and to re-claim
What does the wind know anyway?

history lives in the shadows of the sun ray,
ruins or in the corners of a cave
Ubiquitous, watching from every which way

the eye of a bird on its way
seeking its next perch on which to wait
What does the wind know anyway?
Ubiquitous, watching from every which way.

Caged

When I write in form,
it's easier to capture
the beauty in a leaf
        simplicity in a breeze;

i imagine that it would be nice
to watch the Yellow wagtails
while writing Villanelles in Italy,

remark on the beauty of Sonnets in England,
an occasional Red grouse at my feet
wanting bread crumbs,

or to sketch out a Haiku in Japan —
at a pond under Cherry Blossom,

writing in free verse
it's hard conceal the rage

speaking in Kwansaba —

where they remind me of my place
that always lets me know that I'm
not a bird, but some *thing* other
bound to the ground, wings clipped
where i cannot jump from this, trap
looking to the sky with green eyes
flutter, flight, how so moves the clouds.

jason vasser-elong

Animal

for Tim Siebles

The world is a fast place
before one knows —
its passed them over

a cheetah out chased
by its own desire

Swallows fly further and further south
looking for warmth
finding themselves back in the north
circling a moving circle

and time is carried
by those who keep it
close to the pulse
or dangling from their ribs

Black in February

For 28 days, i get to wear every dashiki i own,
eat Fu-Fu and Cassava — watch Roots
        and be reminded,

bend the spine of dem books bought back in June.

For a few weeks, i get to be African again
while i'm Black year round

so why is it safe to be me
every year around — or after snow
when it's way too cold
to wear Dashikis?

my Cameroonian blood runs warm
my Portuguese blood runs warm
my Spanish blood runs warm
my Netherlandic blood runs warm
my English blood runs warm
my American blood runs warm

and the rivers within lead to oceans of time
say, the rivers within lead to oceans of time

that do not recognize if i
have left home yesterday,

last week or if haven't been back
in over two hundred years.

jason vasser-elong

Right here / Right now

Let's pretend it never happened
that right now i am whispering
this poem into your left ear,
your hand on my hand,

Let's make believe
that you are here &
we are both virgins again,

that no other lips have touched
nor have arms been wrapped around
these shoulders, or your waist.

Let the story of our fingers
be written in a language
only they understand,

that truth begins with right here
and right now.

Dog abroad

A Labrador retriever
taken with family
away to say, America,

is still a Labrador retriever
years after generations
have ran and fetched.

The black friend at the party

He was interrupted
explaining
why his Cameroonian — ness
was just as valid while she,

initiated talk of castles
her people in Ireland —
and that she was 1/4th Cherokee,

and all he was doing
was adding to the conversation
you know banter,
back and forth
and so he persisted –
but she cut him off
like a speeding Mazda
with no regard
for where he was coming from
or going to,

and so he stopped,
smiled then turned
toward a woman
singing the blues.

Frankenstein's shadow

How they stare
might as well have iron rods
protruding from my neck
and thick green skin,

but again am i not
the sum of all colors?

The end result from
so many parts of the world
that sat their weight on my chest,
buried their flags in my flesh.

One day they will say
that once there were black men

who graced the world with love,
gave to the world their genius,
& were chased down to be cleansed

to wash away all of the dirt
from their brown hands,

their memory reduced
to a few names and faces
already fading in their antique frames.

jason vasser-elong

City

Under a canopy
maple leaves drape,

their branches bend brown
spines at the end of the song
of summer, and i am
surrounded,

embraced by the city
moving around me.

City traffic,
laughter of friends
in passing, the trickling
fountain nearby—

a welcome constant
in my life;

there are already leaves
on the ground

& right now
i am anticipating a hillside
or a lake that I have never seen,

and other unfamiliar scenic
treasures all of the pleasures
while vacationing

with my lover
who will eventually become my wife,

but for now, it's the light
touching the bricks
on the side of the building,

the symphony of sirens
that have lost their urgency
on a street i've come to know
by touch —

knowing the vagabond
by name; & i trust
that the sun
without fail, will lick
the whole west side of my
courageous city, fighting
within itself
it too finding the beauty within.

jason vasser-elong

Fair trade

The Keurig is not all that bad,
i prefer the motion of baristas
adding that special touch of personality—
selecting a size   waiting.

Appreciating the aroma of coffee beans
swelling within me   hearing
the clank of mugs to spoons,
the machine's sizzling release of steam,
wondering where it all happens.

Winnowing in the flat fields of Ethiopia, Arabica, or Bra-
zil—
the green and red cherries dry in the sun,
their crumbly skins peeled by hands brown like mine
supple, or cracked in age.

Wet grinding in Sumatra, the slick mucilage
is carefully removed, as fingernails would
shells from thickened albus around yokes—
polished to mahogany and then sorted into piles of jute bags.
Their tilling leads to the filling of cups awakening

inviting their lives into our mugs,
making me consciously aware, as i sit—as i sip
peering beyond the bricks & street lamps of Tower Grove
becoming consciously aware of what I'm doing.

Charity

A stack of one's banded by a paper clip
was taken from the Johnston & Murphy shoe box
with the other stacks waiting for more dead men's faces to
be dropped in the whole

taken then placed in the pocket of a coat

to be carried around   i wonder what they say to each
other? —
if charity to them is giving to a black boy panhandling in
the shopping district   or

an old lady with missing teeth standing
too close to the street for reckless drivers to stop in time
for   or

a young man with a story of being kicked by Police every
morning the sun touches
his daughter's face, before they appear from the rear of a
storefront by the dumpster.

Who am i to suggest they wash dishes when there is a sink
full at home.

This little panoply of one dollar bills of charity in the pocket,
my way of giving money to someone who needs more

jason vasser-elong

if only there was a reset button
or if they could take the game out of the slot
and blow in it.

What do you say to a man after seven days of I don't have
from that corner
as you leave the same café?

Labyrinth

Feathers in place of thread
thread thrown to the wind
wind moves sails
sails guide ships carrying bodies black and bleeding
bleeding and black in a field, in a house
house where there are no yams
yams in place of home
home is away
away i am walking
walking a labyrinth alone
alone in labyrinth looking at statues
statues devoid of noses
noses say something
something about faces
faces that remind of loneliness
loneliness is lost in places
places long forgotten by time
time trapped in the hands
hands tied, cannot tread water
water is inevitable
water is inevitable.

jason vasser-elong

On Proverbs 6:6

i sat and watched an ant colony
      quarry the leaf and cigarette butt riddled cracks,

a single discarded pickle sat off like a monument—
they work in the shadow of the table above
their tiny heads,

      must be like a building
      towering, its shadow
      a tree of shade.
      Some carry loads while
      others just move about.
Their building something
or maybe it's already made—

it's the little things
that move me

like the motivation of an ant
moving a mountain of a crumb
with its back.

Legend

for Dr. Ashmore

Maybe the Bonobos will succeed
when it all comes to a head
and Africa welcomes North America
and Europe back to her chest,

memories of voyages lost
to the winds — the temples
will house questions to our writings

as to how communication failed even
the wisest of apes, languages unspoken
but felt in an embrace.

Perhaps, hiding in the forests
where howls will be heard from in the distance
there will be sightings of some missing link
with answers that will go uncounted, a member

confined to the shadows and to the dark.

jason vasser-elong

Sea Monkey

Often the biggest person in the room
is the shrimp

and the smallest one in the room
is the shark.

Sharks seek out their prey
from those unassuming but confident,
and rarely comment to other sharks
about how big they are, it's interesting.

       Also amusing is when
shrimp refuse to entertain sharks
and are deemed to have a complex—
when questioned about their nature.

       i guess there has to be something wrong
if you are unafraid to swim next to giants
and not cower.

Sidewalk garden

for Mom

You, an ocean
open as air
a meadow
with a tree
standing there,

are rain to a flower bed,
sunshine thereafter
the miracle of life
growing beneath concrete

nursing gardens
in places to dangerous
to keep
delicate flowers.

jason vasser-elong

Libation for an unmarked grave

You were thirty pair of hands,
thirty pair of feet, no names
and yet you stayed and worked
near the flooded creek.

You, amber panoply of souls,
whose hearts diastole to drum beats—
I imbibe palm wine
in remembrance of you.

You belong in the memory, safe from sale—
away from the lash and leer,
you were thirty pair of eyes,
thirty pair of nostrils, ears,
that never saw freedom,
or smelled the smoke clear;

but, my love, there is a Cairn that keeps the rain,
somehow your descendants can taste your tears.

Fossil

Waiting for when
my ink won't be black
or bruised
clinging to the white pages—
used like an arrow
pointed at someone
holding a European Long gun
on the banks of a river
that was named
then renamed, only
to be named again

and then released into the air
with death beneath its feathers
or fear collected like nerves
in its obsidian sharp edge

that angle through the air
already thickened with sorrow

but rather aimed at light
beyond the shadow

the spring of life is ease
while winter makes for hard
enjambled lines
devoid of movement
like bones encased in the ground.

jason vasser-elong

From my window

So i'm sitting at my window,
watching the rain fall onto
the city i love,
that only likes me enough
to pretend that we are friends.

i like how the water sounds
sloshing around the street,

how the gray clouds hovering
paint the cityscape in shades
of sleepy and haze. There's
music trickling the drain,
carrying water to the sun soaked
paved, flowerbeds in need of love.

@ the curb, there is a woman
holding a man's hand as they wait
for the bus, her blonde hair sticking
to the sides of her face, looking
into his eyes, his ebony hands
fixed around her,

they seem to dance right there,
under a street light that only
just started to illuminate,
the shadows already forming
as the city has already began to rest

shrimp

& the buildings have already
turned down their beds, as it begins—
& thunder rolls across the sky,
then gray turns blue then blue
becomes night and they are still
there, dancing under a streetlight,
their bus still on its way.

jason vasser-elong

Life's a peach

You ever sink your teeth
into a peach
that reminds you of someone

the way the skin
and its little hairs
tickle sends ripples of touch
& you blush
just thinking of so and so

& without knowing
your tongue touches the soft dimple
you smell it
then you taste it

you remember how sweet life can truly be.

shrimp   143

Acknowledgments

I GIVE HONOR AND PRAISE to the almighty God for bless-
ing me with this life and for my ancestors, specifically Rose
Jones on my mother's side of the family, born in North Car-
olina into slavery in 1810, and Chatty Vasser on my father's
side, born into slavery in Egypt, Mississippi, the year of her
birth is unknown. May the wind find your souls free from
bondage. I want you to know that your sacrifice lives on
through me. This book is a manifestation of how the village
can take ahold of a child and make a rock from a fist of
sand, may my entire family keep my gratitude.

Thank you to my beloved parents, Beverly Cade and
Willie Gene Vasser, Jr. (Dad, may your soul forever rest in
peace). I thank you two for falling in love long enough to
bring me into the world. I want to thank my sisters Jada Bell
and Caitlyn Vasser for holding big brother up when he was
down. To Shelli Vasser Gilliam (what up cuz?) and her hus-
band (for being so gracious) I thank you for your friendship,
guidance, and advice.

shrimp is a culmination of the years in my life that I
questioned myself and the world in which I lived. To my
friends, colleagues and fellow writers at the University of
Missouri — Saint Louis' Master of Fine Arts Program, 2012-
2014, I thank you for your tireless work offering feedback,
asking tough questions and for allowing me read your work
as well. To my mentor Dr. Sheilah Clark–Ekong, I cannot
thank you enough for always being there, for your wisdom,
comradery and tough love when I needed it. To Pamela

Ashmore for always making time. To Shane Seely, man, we did it! I thank you for seeing something in me I did not recognize in myself. A BIG thanks to Gabrielle David for this opportunity to share my work, and add my two cents.

Special thanks to Michael Castro for your friendship and to Mrs. Davis, who introduced me to the work of Paul Lawrence Dunbar while I attended Visual Performing Arts and Marquette Middle School. Who knew that "A Negro Love Song" would change the trajectory of my whole life? And to my beloved, good morning my *love*, I cannot thank you enough for your love. I know God is real, for here we stand like palm trees.

Finally, to you for reading this very personal part of me, I thank you. I hope that something within these pages touched you and changed you as the tide shifts the sand. ✿

"If you think you're too small to make a difference, you haven't spent the night with a mosquito"

—*African Proverb*

NOTES

1. Kunta Kinte is a character in Alex Haley's iconic book *Roots*, first published in 1976 by Dell publishing Company. In a scene in the book, Kunta is whipped by a slaver and was forced to change his name from Kunta Kinte to Toby, at his master's behest.

2. Makossa is a noted Cameroonian popular urban musical style. Like much other late twentieth century music of Sub-Saharan Africa, it uses strong electric bass rhythms and prominent brass. In the 1980s makossa had a wave of mainstream success across Africa and to a lesser extent abroad.

3. The capital of the West Region of Cameroon, in the Bamboutos Mountains.

About the Poet

JASON VASSER-ELONG is a poet and essayist that was born and raised in St. Louis, Missouri, with maternal ancestral roots in Cameroon, Central Africa. He earned a master of fine arts degree in creative writing from the University of Missouri — St. Louis after studying cultural anthropology and presenting his ethnographic research Rhyme and Reason: Poetics as Societal Dialogue. He has an essay "Treading the Atlantic" in the special edition of the Canadian Journal of Netherlandic Studies — Netherlandic Migrations: Narratives from North America and his most recent poetry appears in *Black Lives Have Always Mattered* (2017), edited by Abiodun Oyewole, *Crossing the Divide: From the Poets of Saint Louis* (Vagabond, 2016), and *Unveiling Visions: The Alche-*

my of The Black Imagination (2016). In 2017, he served as the curator for "Context II," an art exhibition at the Foundry Art Center in St. Charles, Missouri, and was featured in the St. Louis Post Dispatch article, "Poetry can be an early form of artistic response to trauma," by Jane Henderson. He recently appeared in "Never Been a Time" a documentary written and produced by Denise Ward Brown, about the East St. Louis riots of 1917 that sparked the civil rights movement. 🦚

Other Books by 2Leaf Press

2LEAF PRESS challenges the status quo by publishing alternative fiction, non-fiction, poetry and bilingual works by activists, academics, poets and authors dedicated to diversity and social justice with scholarship that is accessible to the general public. 2LEAF PRESS produces high quality and beautifully produced hardcover, paperback and ebook formats through our series: *2LP Explorations in Diversity, 2LP University Books, 2LP Classics, 2LP Translations, Nuyorican World Series,* and *2LP Current Affairs, Culture & Politics.* Below is a selection of 2LEAF PRESS' published titles.

2LP EXPLORATIONS IN DIVERSITY

Substance of Fire: Gender and Race in the College Classroom
by Claire Millikin
Foreword by R. Joseph Rodríguez, Afterword by Richard Delgado
Contributed material by Riley Blanks, Blake Calhoun, Rox Trujillo

Black Lives Have Always Mattered
A Collection of Essays, Poems, and Personal Narratives
Edited by Abiodun Oyewole

The Beiging of America:
Personal Narratives about Being Mixed Race in the 21st Century
Edited by Cathy J. Schlund-Vials, Sean Frederick Forbes, Tara Betts
with an Afterword by Heidi Durrow

What Does it Mean to be White in America?
Breaking the White Code of Silence, A Collection of Personal Narratives
Edited by Gabrielle David and Sean Frederick Forbes
Introduction by Debby Irving and Afterword by Tara Betts

2LP UNIVERSITY BOOKS
Designs of Blackness, Mappings in the Literature and
Culture of African Americans
A. Robert Lee
20TH ANNIVERSARY EXPANDED EDITION

2LP CLASSICS
Adventures in Black and White
Edited and with a critical introduction by Tara Betts
by Philippa Duke Schuyler

Monsters: Mary Shelley's Frankenstein and Mathilda
by Mary Shelley, edited by Claire Millikin Raymond

2LP TRANSLATIONS
Birds on the Kiswar Tree
by Odi Gonzales, Translated by Lynn Levin
Bilingual: English/Spanish

Incessant Beauty, A Bilingual Anthology
by Ana Rossetti, Edited and Translated by Carmela Ferradáns
Bilingual: English/Spanish

NUYORICAN WORLD SERIES
Our Nuyorican Thing, The Birth of a Self-Made Identity
by Samuel Carrion Diaz, with an Introduction by Urayoán Noel
Bilingual: English/Spanish

Hey Yo! Yo Soy!, 40 Years of Nuyorican Street Poetry,
The Collected Works of Jesús Papoleto Meléndez
Bilingual: English/Spanish

LITERARY NONFICTION
No Vacancy; Homeless Women in Paradise
by Michael Reid

The Beauty of Being, A Collection of Fables, Short Stories & Essays
by Abiodun Oyewole

WHEREABOUTS: Stepping Out of Place,
An Outside in Literary & Travel Magazine Anthology
Edited by Brandi Dawn Henderson

PLAYS
Rivers of Women, The Play
by Shirley Bradley LeFlore, with photographs by Michael J. Bracey

AUTOBIOGRAPHIES/MEMOIRS/BIOGRAPHIES
Trailblazers, Black Women Who Helped Make America Great
American Firsts/American Icons
by Gabrielle David

Mother of Orphans
The True and Curious Story of Irish Alice, A Colored Man's Widow
by Dedria Humphries Barker

Strength of Soul
by Naomi Raquel Enright

Dream of the Water Children:
Memory and Mourning in the Black Pacific
by Fredrick D. Kakinami Cloyd
Foreword by Velina Hasu Houston, Introduction by Gerald Horne
Edited by Karen Chau

The Fourth Moment: Journeys from the Known to the Unknown, A Memoir
by Carole J. Garrison, Introduction by Sarah Willis

POETRY
PAPOLíTICO, Poems of a Political Persuasion
by Jesús Papoleto Meléndez
with an Introduction by Joel Kovel and DeeDee Halleck

Critics of Mystery Marvel, Collected Poems
by Youssef Alaoui, with an Introduction by Laila Halaby

shrimp
by jason vasser-elong, with an Introduction by Michael Castro
The Revlon Slough, New and Selected Poems
by Ray DiZazzo, with an Introduction by Claire Millikin

Written Eye: Visuals/Verse
by A. Robert Lee

A Country Without Borders: Poems and Stories of Kashmir
by Lalita Pandit Hogan, with an Introduction by Frederick Luis Aldama

Branches of the Tree of Life
The Collected Poems of Abiodun Oyewole 1969-2013
by Abiodun Oyewole, edited by Gabrielle David
with an Introduction by Betty J. Dopson

2Leaf Press is an imprint owned and operated by the Intercultural Alliance of Artists & Scholars, Inc. (IAAS), a NY-based nonprofit organization that publishes and promotes multicultural literature.

NEW YORK
www.2leafpress.org